The Life of Jesus

First published 2018 by Brown Watson
The Old Mill, 76 Fleckney Road
Kibworth Beauchamp
Leicestershire LE8 0HG

ISBN: 978-0-7097-2524-4
© 2018 Brown Watson, England
Printed in Malaysia

Brown Watson
ENGLAND

An angel came to Earth to visit a young woman named Mary. 'You are going to have a baby,' he said. 'He is the Son of God, and you shall call Him Jesus.'

Mary and her husband Joseph had to travel to Bethlehem. It was a long journey, and they had nowhere to stay. A kind man let them sleep in his stable.

That night, Jesus was born. Angels spread
the news to the shepherds in the fields.

A new star shone in the sky. Wise men from afar knew that the Son of God was born on Earth.

Jesus grew up in Nazareth. He worked with Joseph as a carpenter. He was wise and good, and knew much about the ways of God.

When Jesus was 30, He was baptized in the
river Jordan by a man named John. A voice
from heaven announced that Jesus was the
Beloved, the Son of God.

Jesus spent forty days praying in the
desert. He had no food, and was very hungry.
The devil appeared and told Jesus to turn
stones into bread, but Jesus would not.

The devil tempted Jesus two more times, but
Jesus resisted and sent the devil away.
Instead, angels came to help Him.

Back in Galilee, Jesus began to spread the
word of God. Lots of people trusted and
followed Him. Some helped Him teach, and
they were called His disciples.

Many people were amazed to see
Jesus' faith and glory. When the wine at a
wedding ran out, and servants begged Jesus
to help, He turned water into more wine.

One stormy night, Jesus prayed alone before returning to the disciples who were rowing to shore. Jesus calmed the waves and then walked across the sea to reach them.

The disciples were shocked and afraid.
But Jesus reassured them, and continued to
walk across the water with His disciple,
Peter, by His side.

Jesus spread the word of God, and
performed many miracles in His name.
He cured the sick, healed the lame, and
helped the blind to see.

An enormous crowd followed the disciples to listen to Jesus. They had no supper, so Jesus took five loaves and two fish, and used them to feed thousands of people.

Jesus led the disciples Peter, James and
John up a mountain to pray.
Suddenly, Jesus shone with a bright light
and His face glowed like the sun.

God's prophets, Moses and Elijah,
appeared. God once again spoke from
the sky, saying, 'This is my beloved Son,
listen to Him!'

Jesus rode into Jerusalem on a donkey to celebrate the feast of Passover. The priests were afraid of His power, and paid the disciple Judas to help them arrest Him.

Jesus predicted that Peter would also betray Him. Sure enough, Peter pretended three times that he did not know who Jesus was.

Jesus knew that He had to die to make up
for the sins of people on earth.
He called His disciples together for
one last meal.

Together, they ate and drank. Jesus asked
God to bless the bread and wine. He said it
was a reminder of His body and His blood
that he sacrificed for everyone.

Jesus was killed on a cross for claiming to be the Son of God. When He died, the sky went dark and an earthquake shook the ground.

His body was placed in a tomb and covered with a rock. But three days later, His body had gone. God had raised Him from the dead so He could continue teaching God's word.

After forty days, Jesus spoke to His disciples. He told them God's plan was for Jesus to return to heaven.

Then His feet lifted off the ground,
and a cloud carried Him into the sky.